Juli

PUBLISHE
Copyright © 20

No part of this publication

format, by any means, electronic or otherwise, without prior

consent from the copyright owner and publisher of this book.

Introduction

This book contains 60 of my favorite fudge recipe which I know you will find both easy to make and absolutely delicious to eat. Here are just a few guidelines with certain pieces of equipment I suggest you follow to make the process even easier and make sure you get the best results every time.

Saucepan

Do make sure you use a really good saucepan with a heavy base and firm handles that will let you get a great grip. Use a really good sized saucepan here to make sure you keep everything inside the saucepan when the mixture is boiling.

Candy Thermometer

You will definitely need one of these. The mixture has to reach the right temperature and the only way to measure it exactly is to use a thermometer. If it's impossible to get one or you want to get stuck in straightaway it's still possible to use the softball technique described in the book but I would still recommend a thermometer at some point just to make life easier.

Wooden Spoon

Your arms are going to get a bit of a workout with these recipes which is another benefit! You'll need a good and sturdy wooden spoon for all the recipes.

Bowl

For some recipes you will need a couple of these. Make sure they're a good size and are capable of holding boiling hot mixture.

Pan

You will need an 8x8 inch pan for all these recipes. I would strongly advise you to butter the inside and then cover with wax or parchment paper or foil. Leave a little over the edges as it makes it easier to remove the fudge once it has set in the fridge – you can just pull it out via the paper or foil and then cut it up.

Remember it's not difficult to make fudge at all and it always proves very popular with friends and family. Do be careful though when making that you don't rush the process and let things happen gradually while watching the temperature carefully.

Always take great care of course as you are dealing with very hot mixtures. Be organized before you start and make sure you have a clean and clutter-free surface where you can work without being impeded by anything or easily distracted.

I've cooked all of these recipes for my family at various stages and also made many of them as gifts. They look lovely in a little wrapping and make a great present or something to bring along to a party as well. I hope you enjoy making and eating them as much as I have done over the years!

Julie

Contents

Introduction 2
Amaretto Fudge 7
Apple Pie Fudge 8
Brown sugar fudge 9
Butterscotch Fudge 10
Cake Batter Fudge 11
Candy Cane Fudge 12
Cashew Caramel Fudge 13
Caramel Fudge 14
Cherry Fudge 15
Chocolate Banana Fudge 16
Chocolate Chip Cookie Dough Fudge 17
Crispy Fudge 18
Cinnamon Fudge 19
Coconut Rum Fudge 20
Cookies and Cream Oreo Fudge 21
Cookie Dough Fudge 22
Cranberry Fudge 23
Cream Cheese Fudge 24
Duo-Chocolate Fudge 25
Easy Fudge 26
Eggnog Fudge 27
Fantasy Fudge 28
Fruit and Nut Fudge 29
Ginger Fudge 30

Honey Fudge	31
Hot Chili Fudge	32
Irish Cream Truffle Fudge	33
Lemon Fudge	34
Macadamia Nut Fudge	35
Maple Bacon Fudge	36
Maple Blueberry Fudge	37
Maple Fudge	38
Marshmallow Crème Fudge	39
Million Dollar Fudge	40
Mint chocolate chip Fudge	41
Mocha Fudge	42
Nutella Fudge	43
Oat Fudge Bars	44
Old fashioned Chocolate Fudge	45
Orange Fudge	46
Peanut Butter and Honey Fudge	47
Peanut Butter Chocolate Fudge	48
Peanut Butter Fudge	49
Penuche Fudge	50
Peppermint Fudge	51
Pina Colada Fudge	52
Pineapple Fudge	53
Pumpkin Fudge	54
Rainbow Fudge	55
Raspberry Truffle Fudge	56

Red Wine Fudge 57

Rocky Road Fudge..58

Scottish Butter Tablet Fudge...59

Sour Cream Fudge 60

South African Fudge 61

Strawberry Fudge..62

Vanilla Fudge..63

Walnut fudge 64

White Fudge 65

White chocolate and blueberry Fudge 66

Amaretto Fudge

Ingredients

3 cups chocolate chips
1 can (12 ounce) sweetened, condensed milk
2 tablespoons amaretto liqueur
1 teaspoon vanilla extract

Directions

Grease an 8x8 pan with butter or non-stick cooking spray and cover with wax or parchment paper. Melt the chocolate chips in a bowl over a pan of water over medium heat. Add in the milk and stir with a wooden spoon. When fully melted add in the amaretto and the vanilla and combine. Pour the mixture into the 8x8 pan and place in the fridge. When set, remove and cut into squares to serve.

Apple Pie Fudge

Ingredients

¾ cup apple cider
1 ½ cups unsalted butter *[handwritten: 12oz.]*
5 ounces evaporated milk
3 cups granulated sugar
2 cups white chocolate chips
¾ dried apple, diced
1 teaspoon vanilla
1 teaspoon cinnamon
½ teaspoon nutmeg
¼ teaspoon allspice
¼ cup caramel sauce.

Directions

Grease an 8x8 pan with butter or non-stick cooking spray and cover with wax or parchment paper. Add the cider, butter, milk and sugar into a saucepan. Bring to the boil over medium heat and continue to boil for five minutes while stirring. Remove from heat. Add in the chocolate chips, diced apple, vanilla, cinnamon, nutmeg and allspice. Stir until the chocolate has melted. Pour the fudge into the pre-prepared dish. Add the caramel sauce onto the top of the mixture. Place in the fridge to set. Remove and cut into small squares to serve.

Brown sugar fudge

Ingredients

½ cup + 2 tablespoons evaporated milk
2 cups brown sugar
¾ unsalted butter
¼ teaspoon salt
½ teaspoon vanilla extract
1 ¾ powdered sugar
¾ chopped walnuts (optional)

Directions

Add the milk, sugar, butter and salt into your pan. Bring the mixture to a boil stirring with a wooden spoon. Continue to simmer until the candy thermometer reaches 235 degrees F. Remove mixture and add to a bowl. Add the vanilla in and combine (ideally with a hand held mixer to save your arms). Add in the powdered sugar slowly and combine (use a hand held mixer again!). Add in the walnuts now if you would like. Once done add the mixture to an 8x8 pan and place in the fridge until set. Remove and cut into squares to eat.

Butterscotch Fudge

Ingredients

3 cups butterscotch chips
1 cup chopped pecans
1 tablespoon butter
1 can (14 ounces) sweetened condensed milk
1 teaspoon vanilla extract
¼ teaspoon sea salt

Directions

Grease an 8x8 pan with butter or non-stick cooking spray and cover with wax or parchment paper. Toast the pecans either side and remove to the side. Add in the butterscotch chips, butter and milk into your bowl over a pan of water over a low heat. Stir with a wooden spoon until all are melted together. Remove from heat and add in the vanilla and pecans. Add the mixture into you buttered pan and sprinkle with salt. Let it cool down and then add it to the fridge until it sets. Remove and cut into squares to serve.

Cake Batter Fudge

Ingredients

2 cups yellow cake mix
2 cups powdered sugar
½ cup butter
2 tablespoons sprinkles

Directions

Grease an 8x8 pan with butter or non-stick cooking spray and cover with wax or parchment paper. Add the cake mix and powdered sugar into a bowl. Cut the butter up and add it to the bowl. Microwave for two minutes and stir. Add the sprinkles. Pour into the pre-prepared pan and add to the fridge to set. Remove and cut into small squares to serve.

Candy Cane Fudge

Ingredients

8 ounces cream cheese
4 cups powdered sugar
15 ounces white chocolate chips
6 crushed candy canes

Directions

Grease an 8x8 pan with butter or non-stick cooking spray and cover with wax or parchment paper. Beat together the cream cheese and powdered sugar in a large bowl with a handheld mixed ideally. Put it to one side. Melt the chocolate in a bowl over a pan of water while stirring. Remove from heat and pour over the cream cheese mixture. Beat until combined. Pour the mixture into the prepared dish and smooth out with a spatula. Add in the crushed candy cane to the top of the mixture. Allow to cool, then place dish in the fridge to set.

Cashew Caramel Fudge

Ingredients

½ cup butter
1 can (5 ounces) evaporated milk
2 ½ cups sugar
1 package (12 ounces) semisweet chocolate chips
1 jar (7 ounces) marshmallow crème
24 Caramels
¾ cup salted cashew halves
1 teaspoon vanilla extract

Directions

Grease an 8x8 pan with butter or non-stick cooking spray and cover with wax or parchment paper. Add the milk, sugar and butter into a large saucepan. Cook over a medium heat until the sugar has dissolved. Bring to a boil and stir for about 5 minutes. Remove from the heat and add in the chocolate chips and marshmallow crème. Stir until the chocolate has melted. Fold in the caramels. The cashews and vanilla. Pour the mixture into the pan and place in the fridge to set. Remove and cut into squares to serve.

Caramel Fudge

Ingredients

3 cups sugar
1 cup heavy cream
¼ cup butter
2 tablespoons white corn syrup
1/8 teaspoon salt

Directions

Using your heavy pan brown up 1 cup of sugar. Add in the cream, the rest of the sugar, butter syrup and salt. Cook until you reach softball stage. If using a candy thermometer it will be 235 degrees F. Remove from heat and beat until it becomes thick. Butter your 8x8 inch pan, pour in the mixture and place in the fridge until set.

Cherry Fudge

Ingredients

Butter / cooking spray
1 teaspoon almond extract
Maraschino cherry halves (drained
¼ cup evaporated milk
1/3 cup nuts (optional)
3 cups powdered sugar
½ cup dark coca
1/3 cup chopped maraschino cherries
½ cup butter

Directions

Grease an 8x8 pan with butter or non-stick cooking spray and cover with wax or parchment paper.. Melt the butter in the microwave or your pan and add in the powdered sugar, cocoa and evaporated milk until fully combined. Microwave again or cook over medium heat while stirring until the mixture has thickened. Add in the chopped cherries, nuts and almond extract. Spread the mixture into the 8x8 pan and place in the fridge. When fully set remove and cut into squares to serve.

Chocolate Banana Fudge

Ingredients

1 medium ripe banana
½ cup whole milk
2 ¼ cups granulated sugar
½ teaspoon salt
1 ½ cups chocolate chips
8 tablespoons butter, divided
1 cup miniature bananas

Directions

Grease an 8x8 pan with butter or non-stick cooking spray and cover with wax or parchment paper. Mash the banana and add the milk. Add this mixture into a pan with the sugar and salt over medium heat until the sugar dissolves. Bring to the boil until you get to 235 degrees F. Remove the pan and add the chocolate and mini marshmallows. Stir together until the mixture is smooth. Put the fudge into the pre-prepared tin and smooth. Allow to cool and then place in the fridge to set. Remove and cut into squares to serve.

Chocolate Chip Cookie Dough Fudge

Ingredients

Cookie Dough

½ cup butter
¼ cup granulated sugar
¼ cup brown sugar
½ teaspoon vanilla
1/8 teaspoon salt
2 tablespoons half and half
½ cup all-purpose flour

Fudge:

1/3 brown sugar
1/3 cup butter
Pinch of salt
1/3 cup half and half
4-5 cups powdered sugar
1 teaspoon vanilla
½ cup mini chocolate chips

Directions

Grease an 8x8 pan with butter or non-stick cooking spray and cover with wax or parchment paper. Prepare the cookie dough by beating together the butter and sugar until fluffy (about 3 minutes). Beat in the vanilla, salt and half and half. Stir in the flour until everything is incorporated and set the bowl aside.

For the fudge, add together the brown sugar, butter, salt and half and half in a pan. Stir with a wooden spoon over medium heat until the sugar has all dissolved. Remove from the heat and add in the powdered sugar, a cup at a time, until the mixture is smooth and combined. Add in the vanilla. Add the cookie dough to the mixture and stir to combine. Lastly, mix in the chocolate chips. Spread the mixture into the 8x8 dish and add to the fridge to set.

Crispy Fudge

Ingredients

6 cups rice cereal
¾ cup confectioners' sugar
2 cups semi-sweet chocolate chips
½ cup corn syrup
1/3 cup butter
2 teaspoons vanilla extract

Directions

Add the cereal and sugar into a bow and set aside. Add the chocolate chips, corn syrup and butter into a different bowl and microwave for a minute or so until the chocolate has melted. Add in the vanilla and pour over the cereal mix. Place the mixture into a 13 x 9 inch pan (greased with butter) and place in the fridge until set. Remove and cut into squares to serve.

Cinnamon Fudge

Ingredients

3 cups powdered sugar
½ cup unsweetened cocoa
½ teaspoon ground cinnamon
½ cup butter
¼ cup milk
2 teaspoons vanilla extract
1 cup chopped nuts (optional)

Directions

Grease an 8x8 pan with butter or non-stick cooking spray and cover with wax or parchment paper. Mix together the sugar, cocoa and cinnamon in one bowl. In a heavy bottomed saucepan heat the butter and milk together until butter melts. Add the vanilla extract and combine with the sugar. Add the nuts if you like. Place in the 8x8 pan and put into the fridge until set. Remove and cut into squares to serve.

Coconut Rum Fudge

Ingredients

3 cups sugar
1 ¼ cups condensed milk
¼ cup light corn syrup
2 tablespoons butter
2 teaspoons coconut extract
2 teaspoons rum extract
Desiccated coconut

Directions

Grease an 8x8 pan with butter or non-stick cooking spray and cover with wax or parchment paper. Add the sugar, milk, corn syrup and butter to a pan. Cook over medium heat and stir until it comes to the boil. Continue cooking until it reaches 238 degrees F (softball stage). Remove from heat without stirring and let it cool to 110 degrees F. Add in the coconut and rum extract and beat until the sheen is gone. Add to the 8x8 pan and add the coconut on top. Remove when set and cut into squares.

Cookies and Cream Oreo Fudge

Ingredients

18 ounces white chocolate chips
1 can (14 ounces) sweetened, condensed milk
2 ½ cups of crushed Oreos

Directions

Grease an 8x8 pan with butter or non-stick cooking spray and cover with wax or parchment paper. Add the Oreos to a small plastic bag and crush them with a rolling pin. Placing a bowl above water in a pan melt the chocolate chips and the milk together while stirring. Remove from the heat and add in the crushed Oreos. Pour the mixture into the pan and smooth out. Allow to cool down to 110 degrees F and then add to the fridge to set. Remove and cut into squares to serve.

Cookie Dough Fudge

Ingredients

12 tablespoons salted butter
½ cup sweetened condensed milk
¼ cup heavy cream
2 teaspoons vanilla extract
1/3 cup brown sugar
1 ¼ cup all-purpose flour
3 cups powdered sugar
1 cup chocolate chips

Directions

Grease an 8x8 pan with butter or non-stick cooking spray and cover with wax or parchment paper. Mix together the butter, cream and milk. Add in the vanilla and stir. Add brown sugar and stir again to combine all the ingredients. Add the flour and sugar and continue to stir with a mixer or wooden spoon. Add in the chocolate chips and pour into the 8x8 pan. Place into the fridge for about 4 hours, remove and cut into squares to serve.

Cranberry Fudge

Ingredients

Butter / cooking spray
1 ¼ cups frozen cranberries
½ cup light corn syrup
2 cups chocolate chips
½ cup powdered sugar
¼ cup sweetened, evaporated milk
1 teaspoon vanilla extract
½ cup nuts (optional)

Directions

Grease an 8x8 pan with butter or non-stick cooking spray and cover with wax or parchment paper. Add together the cranberries and corn syrup in a pan and bring to a boil. Continue to boil, stirring now and then, until the mixture has reduced. About 5 minutes. Remove from heat and add in the chocolate chips. Stir the mixture until they are fully melted. Add in the sugar, milk and vanilla extract and stir until the mixture thickens. Pour into the 8x8 pan and place in the fridge until set. Cut into squares and serve.

Cream Cheese Fudge

Ingredients

8 ounces cream cheese
4 cups sugar
6 ounces chocolate
1 teaspoon vanilla extract
½ cup chopped nuts (optional)

Directions

Grease an 8x8 pan with butter or non-stick cooking spray and cover with wax or parchment paper. Melt the chocolate carefully in the microwave. Let it cool and add to the cream cheese mixture along with the vanilla extract. Add the nuts now if you have them. Butter the 8x8 pan (or use wax paper) and pour in the mixture. Place in the fridge until set. Remove and cut into squares.

Duo-Chocolate Fudge

Ingredients

1 pound milk chocolate
1 pound semi-sweet chocolate chips
2 ½ tablespoons butter
2 cups marshmallow crème
2 cups chopped walnuts (optional)
1 can (12 ounces) evaporated mil
4 cups white sugar

Directions

Grease an 8x8 pan with butter or non-stick cooking spray and cover with wax or parchment paper. Add the milk chocolate, chocolate chips, butter, marshmallow crème and nuts to a bowl and mix together. Add the milk and sugar to a saucepan and heat over medium heat. Pour the contents of the saucepan over the chocolate mixture and stir with a wooden spoon. Pour the mixture into the pre-prepared pan and smooth out the surface with a spatula. Place in the fridge and remove when set. Cut into small squares to serve.

Easy Fudge

Ingredients

2 cups semisweet chocolate chips
1 can (14 ounce) sweetened condensed milk
1 cup chopped walnuts (optional)
1 teaspoon vanilla extract

Directions

Grease an 8x8 pan with butter or non-stick cooking spray and cover with wax or parchment paper. Melt the chocolate chips and milk together in a bowl above a pan of boiling water. Stir until smooth. Remove, add in nuts if you have them, and the vanilla. Spread into the pre-prepared pan, let it cool and then add to the fridge until set. Remove and cut into squares to serve.

Eggnog Fudge

Ingredients

2 cups granulated sugar
½ cup salted butter
¾ cup eggnog
12 ounces white chocolate chips
½ teaspoon nutmeg
1 jar (7 ounce) marshmallow crème

Directions

Grease an 8x8 pan with butter or non-stick cooking spray and cover with wax or parchment paper. Combine the sugar, butter and eggnog in a saucepan and bring to the boil. Continue boiling and stirring until the temperature reaches 235 degrees F. Remove from heat and stir in the chocolate chips and nutmeg until the chocolate is all melted. Add in the marshmallow crème. Beat until everything is well mixed and then pour into the pre-prepared pan. Let it cool and then place in the fridge until set. Remove when cooled and cut into squares.

Fantasy Fudge

Ingredients

3 cups white sugar
3/3 cup unsalted butter
2/3 cups evaporated milk
1 package (12 ounces) semisweet chocolate chips
1 jar (7 ounce) marshmallow crème
1 cup chopped walnuts
1 teaspoon vanilla extract

Directions

Grease an 8x8 pan with butter or non-stick cooking spray and cover with wax or parchment paper. Add the sugar, butter and milk into a large saucepan. Heat the saucepan over a medium heat and bring to a boil for five minutes. Remove from heat and add in the chocolate chips, stirring until fully melted. Beat in the marshmallow crème, walnuts and vanilla extract. Add to the pre-prepared pan and place in the fridge to set. Once done, remove and cut into squares.

Fruit and Nut Fudge

Ingredients

16 ounces semisweet chocolate chips
1 can sweetened condensed milk
1 teaspoon vanilla
1 cup dried raisins
1 cup dried cranberries
1 cup chopped nuts (your choice)

Directions

Grease an 8x8 pan with butter or non-stick cooking spray and cover with wax or parchment paper. Melt the chocolate with the milk in a bowl over a pan of water stirring until smooth. Add in the vanilla, cranberries and whichever chopped nuts you fancy. Remove from heat and pour the mixture into the pan. Let it cool and add to the fridge until set. Remove and cut into squares to serve.

Ginger Fudge

Ingredients

6 pieces candied ginger
1 ¼ cup milk
2 cups sugar
5 tablespoons butter
¾ cup semi-sweet chocolate chips

Directions

Grease an 8x8 pan with butter or non-stick cooking spray and cover with wax or parchment paper. Chop up the ginger pieces finely. Add the milk, sugar, butter and chocolate chips to a mixing bowl. Add some water to a pan and bring it to the boil. Place the mixing bowl over the pan and heat, while stirring, until the chocolate has melted. Remove from the heat and add the ginger. Give it a stir and then pour into the pan. Place in the fridge until set. Remove and cut into pieces to serve.

Honey Fudge

Ingredients

1 cup brown sugar
1 ½ cups granulated sugar
1 cup heavy cream
2 tablespoons honey
¾ teaspoon sea salt flakes
1 teaspoon vanilla
6 tablespoons unsalted butter

Directions

Grease an 8x8 pan with butter or non-stick cooking spray and cover with wax or parchment paper. Add the sugars, honey, cream, ½ teaspoon salt and vanilla into a saucepan. Place pan over medium heat and whisk until the sugar has all dissolved. Continue to cook until the temperature reaches 235 degrees F. Remove pan from heat and add the butter. Stir until it has all melted and then leave to cool. Pour the mixture into the pre-prepared pan, sprinkle the remaining salt over the top and remove to the fridge. Take it out when set and cut into small squares to serve.

Hot Chili Fudge

Ingredients

3 cups semisweet chocolate chips
3 tablespoons butter
1 can (14 ounces) sweetened, condensed milk
2/3 tablespoons brewed coffee
2 teaspoons ground cinnamon
1/8 teaspoon chili powder
1/8 teaspoon ground pepper
Sea salt

Directions

Grease an 8x8 pan with butter or non-stick cooking spray and cover with wax or parchment paper. Add the chocolate chips, butter, condensed milk and coffee to a mixing bowl. Bring some water in pan to a boil and place the mixing bowl above it. Stir the contents and cook until the chocolate has melted. Add in the cinnamon, chili powder and pepper. Remove from the heat and pour into the pan. Add the salt flakes over the top and place the pan in the fridge until set. Remove and cut into squares to serve.

Irish Cream Truffle Fudge

Ingredients

3 cups semisweet chocolate chips
1 cup white chocolate chips
¼ cup butter
1 cups sugar
1 cup Irish cream liqueur
1 ½ cups chopped nuts
1 cup semisweet chocolate chips
½ cup white chocolate chips
4 tablespoons Irish cream liqueur
2 tablespoons butter

Directions

Grease an 8x8 pan with butter or non-stick cooking spray and cover with wax or parchment paper. Melt together the 3 cups of chocolate chips, the cup of white chocolate chips and the ¼ cup of butter in a bowl over a pan of water over low heat. Add in the sugar and Irish cream until you have a smooth mixture. Add in the nuts and spoon the mixture into the pan. Smooth it out. Now melt the remaining chocolate and remove from the heat. Beat in the butter and Irish cream. Spread this topping over the fudge in the pan. Make sure the fudge has cooled to room temperature. Put the 8x8 pan into the fridge until it is firm. Remove and cut into squares.

Lemon Fudge

Ingredients

6 tablespoons butter, divided
2 packages (12 ounce) white chocolate chips
2/3 cup sweetened condensed milk
2/3 cup marshmallow crème
1 ½ teaspoons lemon extract

Directions

Grease an 8x8 pan with butter or non-stick cooking spray and cover with wax or parchment paper. Melt the chips together with butter in a bowl of water over a pan or in the microwave until the chips are melted. Add in the marshmallow crème and lemon extract and stir until smooth. Place mixture in the pan and add to the fridge to set. Remove and cut into squares.

Macadamia Nut Fudge

Ingredients

2 cups sugar
½ cup milk
½ teaspoon vanilla extract
½ cup unsalted butter
¾ cup marshmallow crème
1 package (12 ounce) milk chocolate chips
2 cups chopped macadamia nuts

Directions

Grease an 8x8 pan with butter or non-stick cooking spray and cover with wax or parchment paper. Add the sugar, milk, vanilla and butter to a large saucepan. Place over a medium heat until the temperatures reaches 235 degrees F. Remove from heat and add in the marshmallow crème and fold in the chocolate chips. Now add in most of the chopped nuts. Leave to cool to room temperature. Pour into the 8x8 pan and add the remaining nuts onto the top. Place in the fridge to set. Remove once done and cut into squares to serve.

Maple Bacon Fudge

Ingredients

12 strips of bacon
1 ½ cups semi-sweet chocolate chips
1 can (14 ounce) sweetened condensed milk
4 tablespoons unsalted butter
½ teaspoon maple syrup

Directions

Grease an 8x8 pan with butter or non-stick cooking spray and cover with wax or parchment paper. Cook the bacon until it has fully crisped up on both sides. Cut the bacon into small pieces. Add the chocolate chips, milk, butter and maple syrup into a mixing bowl. Add some water into a pan and bring it to the boil. Place the mixing bowl over the pan and stir until the chocolate has fully melted. Remove from the heat and stir in the bacon. Pour the mixture into the pre-prepared pan. Place in the fridge until set. Remove and cut into squares to serve.

Maple Blueberry Fudge

Ingredients

3 cups sugar
1 ¼ cups milk
¼ cup light corn syrup
2 tablespoons butter
2 teaspoons maple syrup
½ blueberries

Directions

Grease an 8x8 pan with butter or non-stick cooking spray and cover with wax or parchment paper. Crush the blueberries with a fork and set aside. Add the sugar, milk, corn syrup and butter together in pan over medium heat. Cook until it reaches 235 degrees F or soft ball stage. Remove from the heat and let it cool to room temperature. Add in the maple syrup and crushed blueberries. Beat until the gloss has gone and pour into the 8x8 pan. Add to fridge to set. Remove and cut into squares to serve.

Maple Fudge

Ingredients

2 cups maple syrup
1 tablespoon light corn syrup
¾ cups heavy cream
1 teaspoon vanilla
½ chopped nuts (optional)

Directions

Add the maple syrup and corn syrup to your heavy bottomed pan. Add the cream and whisk together. Boil until you reach 235 degrees F or softball stage at which point remove from the heat to let it cool down. Pour into a large bowl and beat until it thickens, ideally with a hand-held mixer rather than your arms. Add in the vanilla and nuts if you like. Butter the 8x8 pan and put the mixture in evenly. Place in the fridge until set. Remove and cut into squares.

Marshmallow Crème Fudge

Ingredients

3 cups sugar
1 cup evaporated milk
1 7 ounce jar marshmallow crème
¼ stick butter
1 package (12 ounces) chocolate chips
1 cup chopped nuts (optional)

Directions

Mix together the sugar, milk and butter and cook in a pan until it comes to a boil. Continue to simmer until the thermometer reaches 235 degrees F. Remove from heat, add in the chocolate chips and beat with a handheld mixer until mixture thickens. Add into 8x8 inch (buttered) pan and place in fridge until set. Remove fudge and cut into squares to serve.

Million Dollar Fudge

Ingredients

½ cup butter
4 ½ cups sugar
1 can (12 ounces) evaporated milk
3 packages (12 ounces) chocolate chips
1 jar (7 ounces) marshmallow crème
3 cups chopped nuts
1 teaspoon salt
1 teaspoon vanilla

Directions

Grease a large tin (13x9 inch would be ideal) with butter and add wax paper. Add the butter, sugar and milk to pan and bring to the boil. Boil for about 5 minutes and then remove from heat. Add in the chocolate chips straightway until they melt. Now add in all the remaining ingredients and beat with a wooden spoon until combined. Pour the mixture into the pan and place in the fridge. Allow it to cool and then cut into squares to serve.

Mint chocolate chip Fudge

Ingredients

2 ½ cups white chocolate chips
1 can (14 ounce) sweetened condensed milk
2 teaspoons peppermint extract
6-8 drops green food coloring
2 cups semisweet chocolate chips

Directions

Grease an 8x8 pan with butter or non-stick cooking spray and cover with wax or parchment paper. Melt the chocolate chips in the microwave or in a bowl over a pan of water with the condensed milk. Add in the peppermint extract and food coloring and then fold in the semisweet chocolate chips. Let it cool down and then add to the fridge until it sets. Remove and cut into squares to serve.

Mocha Fudge

Ingredients

2 cans (14 ounce) sweetened condensed milk
1 ½ pounds bittersweet chocolate, chopped
1 tablespoon instant espresso powder
½ teaspoon fine salt
1 teaspoon vanilla extract
1 teaspoon of flaked sea salt

Directions

Grease an 8x8 pan with butter or non-stick cooking spray and cover with wax or parchment paper. Put the milk, chocolate, espresso powder and fine salt into your saucepan over a low heat. Stir with a wooden spoon until the chocolate has melted. Add in the vanilla. Place the mixture into the pre-pared 8x8 pan and place in the fridge. Remove when set and cut into squares to serve.

Nutella Fudge

Ingredients

1 cup Nutella
1 cup salted butter
1 teaspoon vanilla extract
¼ teaspoon salt
4 cups confectioners' sugar
¾ cups chopped nuts

Directions

Grease an 8x8 pan with butter or non-stick cooking spray and cover with wax or parchment paper. Melt the Nutella and butter in a large bowl in the microwave stirring every 30 seconds or so until everything is melted. Remove the bowl and stir in the vanilla and salt. Sift the sugar and add it to the bowl. Add nuts of your choice (e.g. walnuts) if you would like. Put the mixture into the pan, smooth it out and place in the fridge until set. Remove and cut into small pieces to serve.

Oat Fudge Bars

Ingredients

1 cup sugar
1 cup brown sugar
1 cup butter
2 eggs
2 cups flour
1 teaspoon baking soda
3 cups oats
1 cup sweetened condensed milk
2 cups chocolate chips
½ cup butter
1 teaspoon vanilla

Directions

Grease an 8x8 pan with butter or non-stick cooking spray and cover with wax or parchment paper. Combine the butter sugar and eggs. In a different bowl mix together the flour, baking soda and oats and add to the butter mix. Put ¾ of this combined mixture into the prepared pan. Add together the condensed milk, chocolate chips, butter and vanilla. Bring some water to a boil in a pan and place the chocolate mix above it. Stir until the chocolate has melted. Remove from the heat and pour over the mixture in the pan. Add the remaining ¼ of the mixture over the top of the pan. Bake at 350 degrees F for 20 minutes.

Old fashioned Chocolate Fudge

Ingredients

½ cup cocoa
2 cups white sugar
1 cup milk
4 tablespoons butter
1 teaspoon vanilla extract

Directions

Grease an 8x8 pan with butter or non-stick cooking spray and cover with wax or parchment paper. Add the sugar, cocoa and milk together in a saucepan and bring to the boil, stirring with a wooden spoon. Once it starts boiling, reduce the heat. Cook until it reaches 235 degrees F or softball. Remove the mixture from the heat and add in the butter and vanilla extract. Beat together with a wooden spoon until it thickens and loses its sheen. Pour into the pan and, once cooled, place in the fridge, until fully set. Remove and cut into squares to serve.

Orange Fudge

Ingredients

2 cups sugar
¾ cup milk
2 tablespoons light corn syrup
1 tablespoon butter
1 tablespoon grated orange peel
2 tablespoons orange juice
1 tablespoon orange extract

Directions

Grease an 8x8 pan with butter or non-stick cooking spray and cover with wax or parchment paper. Add the sugar, milk, corn syrup, 1 tablespoon of butter and the orange peel into your heavy saucepan. Cook on medium heat until the sugar is dissolved. Carry on cooking, stirring with a wooden spoon, until you reach 235 degrees F. Remove and let it cool down (without stirring now) to about 120 degrees F. Add the orange juice and extract and beat with a wooden spoon or mix with hand mixed until it thickens. Place into the 8x8 pan and put it in the fridge until set. Remove and cut into squares to serve.

Peanut Butter and Honey Fudge

Ingredients

1 cup peanut butter
¾ cup honey
½ cup of chocolate chips (dark or milk)
Sea salt

Directions

Grease an 8x8 pan with butter or non-stick cooking spray and cover with wax or parchment paper. Add the peanut butter, honey and chocolate chips into a saucepan and heat in a bowl over water in a pan until the chips are melted. Remove from the heat and add to the 8x8 pan. Add the salt on top and place in fridge until set.

Peanut Butter Chocolate Fudge

Ingredients

3 cups white sugar
1 cup evaporated milk
¼ cup coca
½ cup peanut butter
1 tablespoon margarine
1 tablespoon butter

Directions

Grease an 8x8 pan with butter or non-stick cooking spray and cover with wax or parchment paper. Add together the sugar, milk and cocoa into a saucepan and stir over medium heat. Keep going until it reaches 238 degrees F (soft ball stage).

Remove from the heat and add the peanut butter and margarine. Beat with a wooden spoon and pour into the pan. Let it cool and then add to the fridge to set. Remove and cut into squares to serve.

Peanut Butter Fudge

Ingredients

8 ounces unsalted butter
1 cup smooth peanut butter
1 teaspoon vanilla extract
1 pound powdered sugar

Directions

Add the butter and peanut butter into a large bowl and microwave for 2 minutes. Remove, stir and microwave for a further two minutes. Now add in the vanilla and powdered sugar to the bowl and combine all the ingredients with a long wooden spoon. Butter the 8x8 inch pan, pour in the mixture and put in the fridge until set.

Penuche Fudge

Ingredients

¼ cup butter divided
2 cups packed brown sugar
1 cup sugar
¾ cup milk
2 tablespoons light corn syrup
1/8 teaspoon salt
1 teaspoon vanilla extract
1 cup chopped walnuts

Directions

Grease an 8x8 pan with butter or non-stick cooking spray and cover with wax or parchment paper. Combine the sugar, milk, corn syrup and salt in a large saucepan. Bring to a boil until the temperature reaches 235 degrees. Remove from the heat and add the vanilla and butter. Let it cool to 110 degrees F and then beat with a wooden spoon until it thickens. Add walnuts and continue to beat until the sheen has gone. Spread the mixture into the pre-prepared pan. Remove to fridge until it all sets. Remove and cut into squares to serve.

Peppermint Fudge

Ingredients

Butter / cooking spray
3 cups semisweet chocolate chips
1 can (14 ounce) sweetened condensed milk
Various peppermint candies of your choice (green and white or red and white look great)

Directions

Grease an 8x8 pan with butter or non-stick cooking spray and cover with wax or parchment paper. Add the chocolate chips and sweetened condensed milk into your cooking pan until the chocolate has melted. Pour into the pan, add in the various peppermint candies and move the 8x8 pan into the fridge. Remove when set and cut into lovely, small squares to serve.

Pina Colada Fudge

Ingredients

2 cups white chocolate chips
1 cup shredded coconut
4 tablespoons butter
¾ cup sweetened condensed milk
¾ marshmallow fluff
½ teaspoon salt
¾ teaspoon coconut extract
¾ rum extract
¾ teaspoon pineapple extract or dried, chopped pineapple

Directions

Grease an 8x8 pan with butter or non-stick cooking spray and cover with wax or parchment paper. Melt the chocolate chips in a microwave stirring every 30 seconds until melted. Stir in the coconut, butter, milk, fluff, salt and extracts and make sure they are well combined. Now add in the dried pineapple if you prefer to use that. Put the mixture into the 8x8 pan and smooth it out if you prefer a smooth top. Once it has cooled to room temperature, put the pan in the fridge until set. Remove and cut into squares to serve.

Pineapple Fudge

Ingredients

Butter / cooking spray
3 tablespoons butter
3 cups sugar
1 can (16 ounces) crushed, drained pineapple
½ heavy cream
1 tablespoon light corn syrup
½ teaspoon vanilla extract
1 cup chopped nuts (optional)
1 drop yellow food coloring

Directions

Grease an 8x8 pan with butter or non-stick cooking spray and cover with wax or parchment paper. Add the sugar, cream, pineapple and corn syrup to your saucepan. Cook until you reach 235 degrees F (or softball stage). Remove from the heat and without stirring, add the remaining butter. Let it cool down now to room temperature. Beat, with a wooden spoon, until it is thick. Add in the nuts and food coloring if you like and spread into the 8x8 pan. Leave the mixture to become firm and then cut into small squares to serve.

Pumpkin Fudge

Ingredients

3 cups sugar
¾ cup butter
2/3 cup evaporated milk
½ cup canned pumpkin
2 tablespoons corn syrup
1 teaspoon pumpkin pie spice
1 (12 ounce) package of while chocolate chips
1 (7 ounce) jar marshmallow crème
1 cup chopped nuts
1 teaspoon vanilla extract

Directions

Grease an 8x8 pan with butter or non-stick cooking spray and cover with wax or parchment paper.. Add together the sugar, butter, milk, pumpkin, corn syrup and pie spice into a saucepan and bring to the boil. Continue to stir until the temperature reaches 235 degrees F (soft-ball stage). Remove from the heat and stir in the rest of the ingredients. Pour into the 8x8 pan and place in the fridge until set. Remove and cut into squares to serve.

Rainbow Fudge

Ingredients

6 cups white chocolate chips
3 cans (14 ounce) sweetened, condensed milk
Food coloring

Directions

Pour a cup of the chocolate chips into a bowl with ½ a cup of the condensed milk into a mixing bowl. Melt in the microwave for about 2 minutes, stirring every 30 seconds. Remove and add a teaspoon of purple food coloring. Whisk around until the color is even. Prepare a baking dish (loaf of bread size) by buttering the inside and then covering with foil or parchment or wax paper. Pour in the mixture and add to the fridge for about 15 minutes. Repeat the process another 5 times – use whatever colors you like – the greater the contrast the better it looks. Finally, just cut up into small squares and serve.

Raspberry Truffle Fudge

Ingredients

3 cups semi-sweet chocolate chips
1 can (14 ounce) sweetened condensed milk
1 ½ teaspoons vanilla extract
¼ cup heavy cream
¼ cup raspberry liqueur
2 cups semi-sweet chocolate chips

Directions

Grease an 8x8 pan with butter or non-stick cooking spray and cover with wax or parchment paper. Combine the 3 cups of chocolate chips and condensed milk and heat in the microwave until melted. Check every 30 seconds and stir with a wooden spoon. Add in the vanilla and salt. Spread the mixture into the 8x8 pan and allow to cool.

In a different bowl add the cream, liqueur and 2 cups of chocolate chips. Heat in microwave until chocolate melts, checking every 30 seconds and stirring with a wooden soon. Remove and let cool until lukewarm. Pour this mixture over the fudge layer. Place in fridge until set. Remove and cut into squares for serving.

Red Wine Fudge

Ingredients

1 can (14 ounce) sweetened condensed milk
1 pound dark chocolate chips
2 tablespoons red wine
2 teaspoons vanilla extract
¼ teaspoon cinnamon
¼ teaspoon salt

Directions

Grease an 8x8 pan with butter or non-stick cooking spray and cover with wax or parchment paper. Put all the ingredients into a bowl and microwave for 2 minutes, stirring every 30 seconds. Remove and stir until the chocolate has melted and the mixture has thickened. Pour the fudge into the pre-prepared pan and smooth the top with a spatula. Place in the fridge to set. Remove and cut into squares to serve.

Rocky Road Fudge

Ingredients

½ cup unsalted butter, divided
1 cup evaporated milk
1 ½ cups sugar
¼ teaspoon salt
12 ounces semisweet chocolate, chopped
½ cup slivered, toasted almonds
1 cup mini marshmallows

Directions

Grease an 8x8 pan with butter or non-stick cooking spray and cover with wax or parchment paper. Add together the butter, milk, sugar and salt in a saucepan. Bring the boil for about 7 minutes while stirring with a wooden spoon. Remove from the heat and stir in the chocolate chips. Fold in the almonds and marshmallows. Pour the mixture into the 8x8 pan. Let it cool down and then add to the fridge until firm. Remove and cut into pieces.

Scottish Butter Tablet Fudge

Ingredients

1 can (14 ounce) sweetened condensed milk
1 cup milk
4 ½ cups white sugar
½ cup unsalted, cubed butter
Dash of salt
1 teaspoon vanilla extract

Directions

Grease an 8x8 pan with butter or non-stick cooking spray and cover with wax or parchment paper. Add the condensed milk, cream, sugar, salt and butter into a saucepan and stir together. Place over a medium heat and bring to the boil while stirring all the time. Carry on boiling until the temperature reaches 235 degrees F or soft-ball stage. Remove from heat and beat with a wooden spoon until the mixture thickens. Add to the pre-prepared pan and let it cool. Add to the fridge to set. Remove and cut into small squares to serve.

Sour Cream Fudge

Ingredients

¾ sour cream
4 cup milk
2 tablespoons corn syrup
2 tablespoons butter
2 cups sugar
1 teaspoon vanilla
½ cup walnut halves (optional)

Directions

Grease an 8x8 pan with butter or non-stick cooking spray and cover with wax or parchment paper. Add the sour cream, milk, corn syrup, butter and sugar into a saucepan. Cook over a medium heat until boiling point is reached. Carry on cooking until the temperatures reaches 235 degrees F or soft-ball stage. Remove from heat and let it cool. Add the vanilla and beat the mixture until it thickens. Pour into the pre-prepared pan and place in the fridge to set. Remove and cut into squares to serve.

South African Fudge

Ingredients

2 cups sugar
5 tablespoons water
4 tablespoons unsalted butter
2 tablespoons Golden Syrup (or dark corn syrup)
1 can (14 ounce) sweetened condensed milk
½ teaspoon salt
1 teaspoon vanilla extract

Directions

Grease an 8x8 pan with butter or non-stick cooking spray and cover with wax or parchment paper. Dissolve the sugar into the water over a low heat. Add the butter and golden syrup and stir until the butter has melted. Add the salt and milk and bring to a boil. Continue cooking until the temperature reaches 235 degrees F or soft-ball stage. Remove from the heat, add the vanilla extract and stir with a wooden spoon until it thickens. Pour the mixture into the 8x8 pan and add to the fridge or leave out to set. Cut into squares to serve.

Strawberry Fudge

Ingredients

1 packet strawberry frosting
1 12 ounce packet white chocolate
Butter for pan
Decorations (optional)

Directions

Butter or line your 8x8 pan with butter. Put the white chocolate into a bowl and microwave until it is melted. Check every 30 seconds and stir with a wooden spoon. Mix in the frosting until well combined. Spread in the buttered pan and add decorations if you wish. Place 8x8 pan in the fridge until set. Remove and cut into squares.

Vanilla Fudge

Ingredients

1 tablespoon butter
3 cups sugar
1 ½ cups heavy cream
¼ cup light corn syrup
¼ teaspoon salt
1 tablespoon vanilla

Directions

Grease an 8x8 pan with butter or non-stick cooking spray and cover with wax or parchment paper. Add sugar, cream, corn syrup and salt to a pan and heat over a medium heat until sugar has melted away. Raise temperature to reach 235 degrees F or softball stage. Remove from the heat and add in the butter and vanilla extract. Let it cool down to about 110 degrees F and then stir with a wooden spoon until the mixture thickens. Add the mixture to the 8x8 pan and place in the fridge until set. Remove and cut into small squares.

Walnut fudge

Ingredients

3 cups semisweet chocolate chips
1 can (14 ounce) sweetened condensed milk
¼ cup butter
1 cup chopped walnuts

Directions

Add the chocolate chips, condensed milk and butter into a large bowl. Microwave until the chocolate chips are melted and then add in the nuts. Grease an 8x8 inch glass baking dish. Pour in mixture and put it in the fridge until set.

White Fudge

Ingredients

2 cups white chocolate chips
2/3 sweetened condensed milk
½ teaspoon vanilla extract

Directions

Butter and line you 8x8 pan. Over a low heat melt the chips in your pan with the milk while stirring with a wooden spoon. Remove from the heat and add the vanilla. Pour into the lined pan and put in the fridge until the mixture sets. Remove and cut into squares.

White chocolate and blueberry Fudge

Ingredients

12 ounces white chocolate
¾ cup sweetened, condensed milk
1 cup chopped almonds
½ cup dried blueberries
1 tablespoon grated orange peel

Directions

Grease an 8x8 pan with butter or non-stick cooking spray and cover with wax or parchment paper. Microwave the chocolate and milk, checking every 30 seconds and giving it a stir. Alternatively melt chocolate in a bowl over water in a pan. Add in the blueberries and orange peel and stir until combined. Pour the mixture into the 8x8 pan and place in the fridge to set. Remove and cut into squares to serve.

Printed in Great Britain
by Amazon